Grace & GRIT

BECOMING A CONFIDENT ENTREPRENEUR

JENNIFER ANN JOHNSON

NAPLES, FL

Copyright © 2024 by Jennifer Johnson
All rights reserved.

Published in the United States by
O'Leary Publishing
www.olearypublishing.com

The views, information, or opinions expressed in this book are solely those of the authors involved and do not necessarily represent those of O'Leary Publishing, LLC.

The author has made every effort possible to ensure the accuracy of the information presented in this book. However, the information herein is sold without warranty, either expressed or implied. Neither the author, publisher, nor any dealer or distributor of this book will be held liable for any damages caused either directly or indirectly by the instructions or information contained in this book. You are encouraged to seek professional advice before taking any action mentioned herein.

All rights reserved. No part of this book may be reproduced or transmitted in any form by any means, electronic, mechanical, photocopy, recording, or other without the prior and express written permission of the author, except for brief cited quotes.

For information on wholesale orders or getting permission for reprints and excerpts, contact: O'Leary Publishing at admin@olearypublishing.com

ISBN: 978-1-952491-72-6 (print)
ISBN: 978-1-952491-73-3 (ebook)
Library of Congress Control Number: 2023921094

Developmental Editing by Heather Davis Desrocher
Line Editing by Boris Boland
Proofreading by Jennifer Doody
Cover and interior design by Jessica Angerstein

Printed in the United States of America

To the bold and brave, the dreamers and the doers,
the ones who dare to step outside the box
and chase their dreams – this book is for you.

CONTENTS

INTRODUCTION – *Living with Grace & Grit* 1

Chapter 1 OUR SECRET SCARS 5
Identify Your Core Values

Chapter 2 THERE IS ALWAYS A PLAN 17
Core Value 1: Have Faith

Chapter 3 IT'S NOT THAT EASY – IN BUSINESS OR LIFE 35
Core Value 2: Inspire

Chapter 4 SLOWING DOWN TO MOVE AHEAD 43
Core Value 3: Know Yourself

Chapter 5 LET GO OF WHAT YOU KNOW 49
Core Value 4: Be Humble

Chapter 6 RISE ABOVE BETRAYAL 55
Core Value 5: Create Honest Relationships

Chapter 7 CHOOSE YOUR COMPANY WISELY 63
Core Value 6: Assume Positive Intent

Chapter 8 GROW FROM SURVIVAL TO SUCCESS 69
Core Value 7: Make It Happen

Chapter 9 ROLE REVERSAL 77
Core Value 8: Own It

Chapter 10 UNFINISHED BUSINESS..83
Core Value 9: Laugh and Have Fun

CONCLUSION - *Looking Back and Moving Ahead*.....................87

ACKNOWLEDGMENTS..91

APPENDIX – *The Grace & Grit Toolkit* 93

ABOUT THE AUTHOR 105

INTRODUCTION

Living with GRACE & GRIT

Let's be real – the entrepreneurial journey isn't all sunshine and rainbows. The gritty moments, the sleepless nights, and tough decisions may feel like they could break you. Racing through business growth without a compass for strategic decision-making can seem like you are on a rollercoaster. Starting, building and growing a business can challenge even the smartest and most capable of us all. It certainly has for me.

So how did I create a successful, thriving business that I love? I have come to believe that things happen **for** me, not **to** me. We can use everything that happens **for** us to guide us. When I look at every single breadcrumb that comes my way each day, I see it through that lens. It is through that lens that I can grant myself that **grace** to live each day as **me,** and find the **grit** to persevere.

I have found that, as an entrepreneur, it goes better when I choose to live with **grace** and with **grit.** I live with **grace** by approaching each day God has granted me with the optimism that I will learn a little and grow a little. Grace means that, in business, I allow myself to not know it all. I allow myself to be curious and to learn. After all, I want to be the best I can be as an entrepreneur and as a human. Grace allows me to be open to gaining knowledge.

I use **grit** every day as well. If I am having a tough day, I look at it this way: God has brought me **to** this, and He will see me **through** this. Whatever the strife is, it will only be temporary. Having grit means that you will go through challenging times, and come out on the other side swinging and better than ever. Grit allows you to adapt, change and become a better version of yourself. In a challenge, we can double our efforts or collapse. Grit allows you to rise to the challenge and fuels you as you move through it.

As I learned to live with grace and grit, I learned that my scars of experience reveal my core values. Knowing your core values is a key to life, because core values guide our thoughts and actions. That is true for all of us, but most of us are unconscious of it. I certainly was. Still, our values guide us, whether we are aware of them or not. What do you value? If you are not sure, your life will show you. Once we become aware of our values, we can use them intentionally in our lives. Our core values are a compass, or a road map for life.

How do we find or clarify our core values? For me, the challenges that I faced showed me where I needed to clarify and/or live by my core values. My experiences were indicators that something important to me (a value or belief) was being squashed. This book is the story of how life helped me clarify my core values – my guiding principles – and how I moved from survival to success. I will share each of my core values as a way to help you define and clarify yours. Once you have clarified your core values, they will guide you in every interaction and experience in life.

This book is a roadmap to becoming a confident entrepreneur. It's filled with stories, strategies, and practical advice to help you overcome your self-doubt, build your confidence, and create the business of your dreams. I want you to know that you are not alone. I've been there. I know that self-doubt and the fear of failure that can hold you back. But I also know that you are capable of anything you set your mind to.

So, go forth and be bold! Believe in yourself and your dreams, and know that I'm cheering you on every step of the way.

I have not always lived with Grace & Grit; nor did I live by my core values. There was a time that I came very close to dying because I didn't, and that is where we will start.

1 Our secret SCARS

What does it mean to "identify your core values?" And how does that apply to becoming a confident entrepreneur? As we start our journey together, I want to ask you a few questions to help you see if you are aware of your core values, and to find out if they take priority in your decision-making for your growing business.

- Are you familiar with that recurring feeling of trying to be everything to everyone?
- Do you often do things that you don't want to do, in order to support others?
- Do you give time or money to people or organizations out of guilt?
- Do you look at others who seemingly have it together, and think that "someday soon" it will slow down for you and things will change?

- Do you find that you have no time for yourself; that your business's growth is taking over your life?
- Do you want to grow your business, but don't see a way to do it, given the amount of time and energy you are already expending?
- Would you love to be able to step away from your business for a month and know that it is still running as efficiently as it was when you were there?

Growing a successful business is a struggle that many of us can relate to. We may not realize that a lack of awareness of our core values is a reason for our business's stalled growth; however, I would say that it is probably the most fundamental reason that businesses fail. The owner is not following their own core values, and becomes so burned out that he or she just can not do it anymore. The profits don't bring happiness, and the time spent is too costly.

Five years ago, I was lost. I felt like I had been on autopilot. I wondered: *Am I still on the right path, or am I just going in circles?* It was scary; I won't lie. But instead of staying stuck in the confusion, I did something crazy. I grabbed a pen and started journaling – digging deeply into the stuff that really mattered to me. I wrote about ideas that made my soul tingle, values that were part of my personal compass, and even weird, fleeting thoughts that danced like fireflies in my head. Every time a thought popped up, I would write it down on paper. And it was hard! At first, I felt like I was searching for buried treasure, blindfolded. I thought: *What am I even looking for? How is it supposed to feel?* But slowly, with every scribble, it started to click.

My journal became a mirror – reflecting who I was, and who I was not. Writing helped me uncover hidden passions, untangle confusing priorities, and rediscover the things that truly make me tick. It was not always easy, but each page turned was a step closer to finding myself.

As I wrote and discovered more of who I was at my core – and found what really mattered to me – I started to group together the pieces that really spoke to me. Eventually, I had nine groups; each with a heading. These were my core values. The crisis that I was in led me to clarify those values. And going forward, that clarity powered my businesses. Describing my core values was a key turning point in my success as an entrepreneur and business person.

So, if you are feeling lost in the maze of life, grab a pen and start writing. It might not give you all the answers right away, but trust me, it's a journey worth taking. You might just surprise yourself with what you find along the way.

In working with entrepreneurs – and in my own experience – I have found that our lack of clarity around core values traces back to experiences we had as youths, or from early career choices. The ambiguity might have surfaced during a past relationship or might have been tied to an unresolved issue that left us questioning our skills – or worse yet, questioning our worthiness for success. This relentless pursuit of "**doing more**" and "**being more**" often leads to exhaustion, and it's crucial to understand where the issue originates.

It first showed up for me as a teenager when I got into a bad relationship and didn't know what to do. I was young and hadn't had time to develop my life philosophy. As I reflect on that time, and share it here with you, I want you to think about your own past. Try to see where you might have experienced less-than-ideal circumstances because you didn't have a core-value compass.

Travel back with me to the early 1990s, when I was a junior in high school in a small town in Minnesota. I was active in many activities; my parents said that I burned the candle at both ends! I was a cheerleader, on the speech team, part of a mock trial team, and in 4-H (I was a farm girl, after all). Plus, I worked at a fast food restaurant.

It was at the restaurant that I met Eric, a co-worker of mine. He was tall and had a black, curly mullet (which were "in" back then). He was a year older than I was. To be honest, I have no idea what attracted me to him. Perhaps it was his humor and how charming he was – or maybe I was attracted to his "bad boy" persona.

At first, I was reluctant to date him. There is something to be said for our intuition, or whispers, as I like to call them. (Pay attention to them.) I finally agreed to date him, and after the second or third date, I began to see signs of controlling behavior.

One evening after a movie, we were taking a drive in his Mustang. I wanted to go home, but he said, "No, I won't let you go home. You have to be with me tonight." I was scared and wanted to get out of the car. I told him that I did not want to see him again and he hit the steering wheel – the old-school Mustang wheel with three spokes.

Eric said, "If you ever say anything like that again, or if you leave me, I will kill you." I looked over at him, and saw that his knuckles were bloody from having struck the steering wheel so hard. Being young and naive, I thought he was just joking about the "killing" part – like it was just a figure of speech.

I had no idea what I had gotten myself into. I can still see and feel that moment as though it happened yesterday.

Well, he wasn't kidding. He was verbally abusive; he called me names and told me that I was ugly and lucky to have him. He told me that I would not be able to find anyone else to love me. Then, the verbal abuse escalated to physical violence. He began hitting me – but in a way that I thought he was just playing rough with me.

Then, one evening, we were in his bedroom, and he accused me of cheating on him with his friend – which I had not. He threw me up against the wall and I almost blacked out. Another time, at work during my lunch break, he grabbed me by the front of my shirt and shoved me up against a large ice machine. My co-workers saw him do it – and they didn't do anything. That made me feel worthless. The truth was that he had cheated on me with a co-worker, which was a blow to my already-low self-esteem when I found out.

I was on a trip for school and I had a sinking feeling, which confused me. I called him and he did not answer, which was unusual. When I got home, I found out that he cheated on me while I was away. Our intuition is powerful. It took me a long time to learn to listen to those *whispers*.

The violence continued. He slapped me, kicked me, and forced me to have sex. One night I was at his house and he got carried away. He took a pillow and put it over my face; he tried to smother me. I don't recall why he did it; perhaps I didn't comply with something he wanted me to do.

After each violent act, he promised he would never do it again. He would be sweet and loving to me, giving me presents. But he also blamed me, and told me that I had been asking for it. Eventually, I told my best friend about the violence; she urged me to leave him. Which I did not do.

It took a long time before I told my parents about any of it. When I did, I only described a small part of what was actually happening. I was too ashamed. They supported me and told me that I did not deserve to be treated that way; they encouraged me to report the incidents to the police. But it was a small town in Minnesota, and everyone knew everyone else's business. I was afraid of being humiliated.

Eric brainwashed me to believe everything he was saying. To an outsider, it might be hard to understand why I would choose to stay in a violent situation. I know there were plenty of people rolling their eyes. I stayed for a few reasons: I didn't think that I could do any better; I thought he would hurt me and my family; and finally, I thought I could change him. (That does not work.) When he asked me to marry him, I said "yes." Heck, I even bought the ring! Go ahead and roll your eyes.

The relationship with Eric even stopped me from pursuing my dreams. From the time I was young, I had dreamed of being a TV anchor or talk-show host. I knew that God put me on this earth to do that. I was able to earn a scholarship to go to college for a degree in broadcast journalism; however, Eric told me that if I went, he would kill not only me but my family as well. So, I did not go, and my dreams of being a TV news anchor went out the door.

The final straw for me came one cold winter evening. There was not much to do in the small town where we lived, so we would get in our cars and cruise up and down Main Street at night. One night we were doing just that, and we stopped in the parking lot of a pharmacy that was closed. I said something that Eric did not like – and in front of his friends. He knocked me down and I fell on the ice. His friends finally saw the truth; even so, they turned a blind eye.

I broke up with him and told him I did not want to see him again. I even gave him the engagement ring; I thought it was finally over. Well, it wasn't. Abusers do not give up without a fight. For months after our breakup, he stalked me. He would follow me home or try to drive me off the road. On one occasion, he forced me off the road and raped me.

He would call our house phone (this was before the days of mobile phones) at all hours of the night to make sure that I was home, and not out with someone else. Finally, I decided that the only way I was going to get out of the situation was to move. And so I moved to a town about two hours away.

About a year after I broke up with Eric and moved away, my new boyfriend (who was wonderful) and I went to a festival in his hometown. Eric was there. When he saw me, he began calling me names and threatened to kill us both. It really scared us. My boyfriend encouraged me to file an order for protection, which I did.

After a few months, we went to court. I was assured that a guy like Eric would never show up for the court hearing. Not only did Eric show up, he showed up **with an attorney** to fight the order. But I was able to get the order for protection, and the nightmare was finally over. That was the last I ever saw of Eric. At the time, I didn't know why I didn't die. Today, I know why.

Looking back, I see that I **lost myself** in the relationship with Eric. I didn't see how much I was giving up for one person – a person who treated me so poorly. And the scars I acquired during that trying time in my life didn't reveal themselves to me for a very long time. When they did, it was frightening and unsettling.

As a result of my time with Eric, I developed fears of water and small space. My fear of water means that I cannot swim with my children. My claustrophobia can be so bad at times that I can't wear tight clothing. I have been known to literally cut a piece of clothing off of myself after trying it on at home, simply because it felt too constraining. Some wounds become scars that influence us for life.

For years, I struggled with how I could have let myself endure such a damaging situation for so long. I eventually realized that I did not know what I valued. I was young, naive and unaware. I had not yet clarified my **core values**. When we do not know who we are or what we stand for, we can easily attract and tolerate the wrong people.

The experience with Eric was the beginning of my realization of how important it is to have **core values** to live by. It started a long process of refining the principles that I live by – the same principles that have helped me to build multiple successful businesses. The first value is to **Have Faith**, and that is where we will start.

LIVING WITH GRACE & GRIT
IDENTIFY YOUR CORE VALUES

Do you ever wonder why certain (especially difficult) things happen to you? You lost that "big client"; you didn't win "that contract"; or, you lost several key employees. I have been there more times than I would like to count. Every time I was frustrated, I wondered: *Why me?* Now I look at everything and see that it is happening **for** me, not **to** me. To handle it all, it takes both grace and grit. In each hand we are dealt, there is a lesson – a chance to learn, change, and become a better version of ourselves. We can wallow in misfortune and become a victim of our circumstances; or, we can use them to learn, grow and be better. We can even use our triumph over circumstance to help others. So, when things are hard or confusing, ask yourself, *Why is this a good thing?* The answer just might surprise you.

Start thinking about what you value. Your life will show you what your core values are. Those values are different for all of us, and they are often revealed to us during challenges. Look back on your life, and start to see the clues that indicate what you value most. What principles do you live by? Take time to be still and listen. When you "hear" your values, write them down! Pay attention to your *whispers* – they will help you!

Note: Your values are dynamic – they can evolve and change. It is also normal to add and remove values; they are meant to be fluid. They are there to serve you for a purpose, a reason, or a season. Many times, core values actually overlap, as they are connected and flow from one another.

2 There is always A PLAN

It's easy to get caught up in the whirlwind of daily events, the constant stream of decisions, and the unpredictable twists and turns that make up our day. Amid the chaos, it's natural to question whether there's a guiding force or a master plan for our lives. Kind of like a blueprint.

There is always a plan, even if we don't think there is one, and even if it is not **our** plan. There have been so many times in my life that God has stepped in and said, *This is my plan for you.* He has laid it all out. His voice comes to me as the *whispers* I mentioned before. If you allow yourself to be quiet and still in your being, you will hear these quiet *whispers* in your life as well. We all have them. You may experience a *whisper* as a feeling in your gut, or a quiet voice, or something that happens. These *whispers* have led me to my first core value: **Have Faith.**

I believe in fate and I have faith. I have a higher power and my higher power is God. My higher power brought a man into my life when I was at my lowest. It was a few months after I had broken up with Eric, and I had zero self-esteem. I remember the day I met this man like it was yesterday. It was probably the most important day of my life, and meeting him maybe even saved my life.

It was a Friday. I was walking out of a convenience store in rural Minnesota, on my way to one of my three jobs. I saw a tall man with broad shoulders and sandy blond hair. He was wearing a suit, but what I remember the most was his cute little button nose. As we walked past each other, I thought, *I'm going to marry this guy someday.* I could hear the *whispers* that day and I was listening to them!

The next day I went to my job at a fast-food restaurant (the same place I had met Eric) about 30 miles away from where I had seen the man. I was working at the front counter. I looked up and there was the same man, standing in front of me in all his glory with one of his friends.

I said, "Hey, I saw you yesterday at the gas station." He said that remembered me. I had butterflies in my stomach and tears welling up in my eyes; I could not believe he remembered **me.** His name was Brad, and he had come to town to get aviation fuel for his speed boat. He was even cuter on day two, I thought.

Brad and I struck up a long conversation. He left about an hour later, but returned, coming through the drive-through with his business card.

Meeting Brad allowed me to finally break free from Eric. I would call Brad and he would talk to me at all hours of the night. He would meet me at his house, just to chat. He seemed too good to be true. He was kind, gentle, and spoke to me like I was worth something as a person. He never forced me to do anything – and that included sex.

At one point I asked him what he wanted. I assumed that he had an ulterior motive. But there wasn't; I came to realize that the way he treated me was how a person is supposed to be treated.

Over the next few months, we strengthened our bond. It was about a month after I met him that we started dating and became an "official" couple. We would go out on dates or take his speed boat for rides on the lake where he lived. In the winter, we would go snowmobiling. Honestly, we just hung out and enjoyed each other's company.

God was looking out for me on the day that Brad walked into my life. Brad is what really helped me break away from that previous, horrible relationship; he truly saved my life. He helped me see that most people are not mean and ugly and nasty to each other; rather, they are kind, loving and caring, without expecting something else in return. Brad was and is my everything. He understood me; he cared for me. We had fun together and he loved me.

During the time that Brad and I dated, he started out traveling about two hours to work each day with his family. Brad and his family owned a business in real estate and they worked in Minneapolis. At first, I continued working at an insurance agency as a secretary, but I soon found a position as a leasing agent at an apartment company in St. Cloud, Minnesota, which was about an hour's drive from my house. Brad and I continued seeing each other almost every day.

Finally, after about eight months, we moved into an apartment together in a suburb of Minneapolis. I quickly found my first "big-girl job" and became an office manager at a manufacturer's representative firm for building products. It was at that job I met some of the most kind, caring and beautiful people I could ever hope to meet. The business was operated by a family that was rooted in values, faith in God, and family. Again, God put me **there** for a **reason.** They became an extended family for me. It was while working for that family-owned business that I got the itch to own my own business. I saw how the family all worked together tirelessly to create their own destiny – I wanted to do that too.

It took Brad seven years to ask me to marry him. By that time, we had moved into a house. I am not sure why it took him so long, but he jokingly says that the more I asked him about marriage, the longer it took. Christmas is my favorite time of the year and as it was approaching the holiday season in 2000, Brad had hung a gold wire bell inside our Christmas tree. Inside was an engagement ring for me. On December 22, he finally proposed. When he asked me, I was so shocked. Instead of saying yes, I said, "Are you sure?" Then, I said yes.

The funny thing was, I found out that he actually had the ring for almost a year before he asked me. He had it hidden in our unfinished basement, in the framing of our house. It became our custom to hang that gold wire bell (that my ring was in) on our tree every year.

We were married in July of 2001 in a fairytale wedding at my hometown church with my family and friends. The beautiful stained-glass windows, historic wooden pews, and grand organ set the stage. The day was one of the hottest on record, and the old church didn't have air conditioning. But, it was not the heat I remember. I remember how I felt: overwhelming peace, knowing I had found my soulmate. The experience of finding my soulmate led me to have greater faith.

After Brad and I got married, my desire to start a business became stronger. I felt it in my gut, my bones, my head, **my very being.** I realized I was great at planning my wedding; the whole wedding-planning thing intrigued me. So, I found a place that offered wedding planning courses. Back in the day they sent books to study for courses (there was no online learning). I immersed myself in the books, graduated from the course, and received a certificate for wedding planning.

I opened up Heartstrings Bridal out of my house in 2001.

I hustled. I attended wedding fairs and did anything I could do to drum up business. I was listed in *The Knot* magazine, and in every other possible wedding publication I could find. I started attracting clients. The experience with my first couple was exhilarating; they also brought excited "butterflies" and the "I think I am going to throw up" feeling. But I was tasked with planning their wedding; they hired **me!** Eventually – once the internet became robust – I found myself with a beautiful website and a large online presence.

Not once did I think I could not do it; not once did I think I wasn't qualified. So how could that can-do attitude change from then to now? I think that with time, we allow ourselves to think of all the things that could go wrong, and that trips us up. It allows us to get in our heads and we come up with that "imposter syndrome" mentality. We start talking ourselves into some crazy shit. Back then, I was young, naive and invincible. With age, I am much less so.

After I started Heartstrings Bridal, I just kept on adding brides and grooms. I wanted to be the planner that every bride and groom looked to. But I soon realized that there was a gap – an opportunity – in our industry. At that time, chair covers were the "thing to have" on the chairs at a reception. The covers created a sea of white or ivory, and it made for a great backdrop. I discovered that no one offered chair covers at a reasonable price, so I started offering covers as part of my business. It was very successful. We kept the chair covers on upholstery hangers, which were on rolling racks in the garage. We would rent them out for brides to install themselves, or we would install them.

I would spend countless hours cleaning the covers after they were used. Cleaning them was mundane work, but I was so happy to be able to do it. I was creating my destiny, my future – and it exhilarated me. Every weekend, I would do it all over again. I was growing the business pretty rapidly, to the point that we needed to have a commercial space.

The day I found our home for Heartstrings Bridal comes to mind as though it was yesterday. It was Easter weekend, and I happened to be driving through a nearby small town (Hopkins, a small suburb of Minneapolis). I saw a beautiful old home with an awning for sale; it housed an interior design studio. I called Brad and told him that I wanted to see the house immediately. So we looked at it, purchased it, and moved in a few months later. The house allowed us to begin expanding our business even more; eventually we added a bridal shop and tux rental operation to the mix. I noticed the same kind of "butterflies" as I had when I first started my business. However, I just knew in my gut that **this was it** – **I could** do this, and I **was going** to do this.

We had done a good job growing the bridal business, and it was time to start growing a family. We had been married for a few years and had tried to get pregnant with no success. We prayed and prayed for a baby. I had faith; we did all the treatments that were suggested, including four rounds of in vitro fertilization. I had countless surgeries for endometriosis, and still nothing. It was a very lonely and scary time. *Will I ever be a mom? Am I supposed to be a mom? Why is everyone getting pregnant but me?*

I became angry, frustrated and hopeless. Then, four years to the day after Brad asked me to marry him – on December 22, 2004 – we found out that we were pregnant! Not with just one baby, but with two! We were over the moon. I remember my husband's expression when the doctor told us it was twins ("holy $#*t"). We could not have been more excited! But, things were about to get hard – **really** hard.

A few weeks after we found out that we were pregnant, we started our birthing classes. That day is still so vivid in my mind. The evening when we were coming out of the class, I had the worst crampy pain (like a period, but 100 times worse) that I had ever felt. I ended up in the hospital. At first, they thought I was having appendicitis and did a lot of testing. The doctors determined that I was having premature labor. I jokingly said to the doctor, "Oh my goodness. The birthing class was so traumatic, it put me into premature labor." If you have ever been to a birthing class, you know what I mean. They are enough to send you running!

From that day forward (I was about seven weeks along), I was put on bed rest. I had to be at home in bed or in a hospital for the entire pregnancy. It was the hardest time of my entire life. Up to that point, things had not exactly been smooth sailing, but this was different. It wasn't just me, or my feelings, or my body that I was worried about. I had two tiny babies in me who were depending on **me** to grow them.

On top of the worry was also frustration and anger. Here I was, living the dream – I was finally pregnant. I had a great marriage and I was an entrepreneur who had recently started a business… but **now** I was being robbed of enjoying my pregnancy like a normal woman. I had already been robbed of getting pregnant like a normal woman… and now this. People get pregnant every day and go through nine months of pregnancy and give birth and it all works out. *Why did this have to happen to me and my babies?*

My faith was tested. I asked God, "Why **me?** How does this fit in?" I asked "Why me?" over and over and didn't come up with an answer. "It's not fair" was also a part of my vocabulary for quite a long time. *What did I do wrong?* I kept hearing that God gave us the situation because we could handle it. But I wasn't so sure. *Who does He think I am? I am certainly not ready for this.*

My husband and I ended up moving in with my in-laws because I could not be trusted to stay in bed: I am a doer; I am active! My strong will and busy-beeness has always been a part of me. We even purchased one of those adjustable beds so I would be comfortable. I couldn't even shower without sitting on a chair. I was literally in bed every single day.

The fear was that my babies would come too early. At that time, 28 weeks was considered the earliest a baby could survive; therefore, our goal was to get to at least 28 weeks.

I was in and out of the hospital – more in than out. The contractions would start and not stop and that landed me in the hospital. Imagine having painful contractions for months. Not fun – very scary and stressful. My premature labor was so bad that I had to have a cerclage (my cervix was sewn shut so the babies could not come out). I also had to have a permanent port put in my leg so the hospital staff could administer drugs to stop the contractions.

I was not the easiest person to hang out with during that time. I was angry, frustrated, sad and scared. But one blessing during that time was Brad. I think back to all the days and nights spent in the hospital with fondness. My husband was there with me, and when he wasn't, my mother-in-law would stay with me.

The hospital was prepared for women with complications like mine and they had takeout menus from every restaurant around that would deliver. When I was there, the highlight of the day was take-out! To this day, the smell – or thought – of hospital food is enough to turn my stomach and make me vomit.

When I was able to be at home, I would work on wedding planning from my chair. We had just purchased a brand-new building and opened a bridal shop to add to my services. The whole time I was on bed rest, I wondered how I was ever going to get through it. I would have waves of feeling ungrateful and selfish; I would complain that I had to sit in a chair all day, and that I could not work, and that I had babies inside me that I was trying to keep alive.

Fortunately, my employees stepped in to do the day-to-day work at Heartstrings Bridal. My mother-in-law, who was such a great support for us, even stepped in to take over the planning at a few weddings.

Memorial Day came. I was very agitated and grumpy that day, not feeling well at all. Then, that evening, I started vomiting and felt terrible. Around 1 a.m., we contacted the doctor, and we were advised that I get to the hospital immediately. My husband drove more than 100 mph down the freeway to get me there.

When I arrived at the hospital, they tried to stop the contractions with drugs that were even stronger than the ones I had at home. I had been determined to carry the babies for at least another full week (I was at 27 weeks). But my babies were determined too; "Baby A" had broken through my cerclage and was well on her way. The doctor came in, examined me, and said, "It looks like you are having your babies today."

I looked at her. With all my anger, force, and anything I had left in me, I told her, "No way. You are not getting them today!" She assured me that it wasn't up to me. She said that they would need to do an emergency C-section.

Most of it was a blur. I remember looking at "Baby A" and then looking at "Baby B" (that is what the doctors called them) and then nothing after that. It turned out that "Baby A," our daughter, was born breathing and weighed 1 pound, 13 ounces. But "Baby B," our beautiful son, was not breathing when he was born at 1 pound, 9.5 ounces (the half-ounce counts when a baby is that tiny). Both babies were intubated and taken through an underground tunnel to the Children's Hospital.

I have vivid memories of the nurses wheeling my big hospital bed through the underground tunnel to the Children's Hospital just hours after the twins' birth. There my babies lay, in their incubators. Their little tiny bodies were so small. They looked helpless and innocent. Even though my babies were brand new, they looked so old. That is typical with preemies, because their skin is very thin and wrinkled.

We named them Gracie and Brady. Our little Gracie, who was two minutes older than her brother, was very strong from the beginning. She amazed everybody on the medical team and was off the ventilator within a week. I remember thinking from the minute I met them that she would be OK. I did not worry about her as much as I did about her brother.

When babies are born so early, their lungs are not developed; and unfortunately, it is something that plagues boys more than girls. Brady was the sickest little boy in the NICU. He was so sick that at one point the doctors said that if we believed in God, we should have him baptized.

Sitting there listening to the doctor tell us that was like getting punched in the stomach. I was worried about our little Brady, but how could it be that bad? Nonetheless, we baptized both babies; and within three days, Brady had turned the corner and gained strength. Our little Brady is a fighter. God had plans for him – as he does for all of us!

The days and months that followed were even more harrowing and traumatic than what I had already been through. It was one of the longest journeys I have ever been on. After two weeks, I was released from the hospital; but Brad and I would spend all day there at our babies' bedsides, taking turns watching them. After we went home for the night, I would call their nurses to check on the newborns before I went to bed. And then I would get up in the middle of the night to call again. When I woke up, I would call a third time.

Eventually, Gracie and Brady progressed, grew, and gained weight. Soon, the hospital staff allowed them to lie next to each other. That was the most heartwarming and endearing thing. They would hold hands, cuddle and snuggle. One of the most fascinating things that we did as new parents was what they call Kangaroo Care. We would take our shirts off and let the babies lie down chest-to-chest with us. You could see their heart rates regulate as they calmed down. The staff was usually even able to turn down the twins' oxygen levels while we were doing Kangaroo Care.

Gracie ended up coming home after three months. It took Brady a little longer – he came home at 4 months old. They both came home on heart monitors, and Brady also had a feeding tube. The doctors warned us that no baby had ever gone home on a feeding tube that didn't go back to the hospital within a week. But Brady was the one that proved them wrong. He pulled that feeding tube out about two months after he came home and did not look back. Like I said, he is a fighter.

What we went through to bring Gracie and Brady into the world and keep them alive was the hardest struggle and greatest challenge of my life. The blessing that came out of all of it is that it allowed me to see God's presence in every facet of my life – in my relationships, and in creating and sustaining my babies. God was there with my husband and me, and our two tiny babies. That challenge is where one of my core values, **Have Faith,** revealed itself to me. God was there holding our hands, and guiding us and telling us that our babies would be OK. God had a plan for our babies, as he has plans for all of us. We just have to have the faith to believe.

LIVING WITH GRACE & GRIT
HAVE FAITH

Remember that God always has a plan for us and is guiding us. God put us there in that moment because we would have the strength and belief to get through to the other side after our journey is done. All that is needed is to **Have Faith** in God. I look back at so many areas in my business where I was pulled in a different direction. I always wanted to own a clothing store, but everything I was doing as a business owner seemed to move further away from that. All the other businesses I was in eventually prepared me for where I am now... owning a clothing store!

We have to be still and know that we are being guided. We can be that example, that North Star, for someone else who is going through something similar. I remember so many things from my pregnancy journey, and when I hear of someone else going through something similar, I can empathize with them. I understand what they are facing. I can be there to let them know that there is hope for them; that miracles can happen. You just must Have Faith.

PRACTICE THIS CORE VALUE

A practical way to practice **having faith** is to try to **live in the present** as much as you can. Pray, meditate, make a list of what you are grateful for – or, just slow down and step back to see what is set out in front of you. Here are a few questions you may ask yourself that can help you harness the moment of **now.**

1. What am I feeling? How do I feel physically and emotionally, and what are my thoughts?
2. Use your senses: What am I seeing, hearing, smelling, tasting, touching?
3. Am I rushing from one task to the next?
4. Am I doing something mind-numbing, like endlessly scrolling through social media?
5. Am I engaged in what is happening around me right now?

3 It's Not That Easy IN BUSINESS OR LIFE

*H*ave you been there? Feeling lost, alone, and defeated? The weight of the world on your shoulders? I've been there too.

Business is full of challenges. It's a relentless roller coaster of triumphs and setbacks; a never-ending battle against uncertainty and doubt. It's a test of your resilience, your creativity, your very soul. There will be times when you feel you are lost, alone and defeated.

But it's also an incredible journey of growth, of learning, of shaping something from nothing. It's the thrill of the chase, the satisfaction of achievement, the joy of making a difference.

Looking back at my life, I can see clearly the areas where life was happening **for** me and not **to** me. I was learning valuable skills that I could use in other areas of my future life. I must say that the realization did not come quickly or easily, but it did come. It came to me when I became open to it and still enough to actually hear the message.

People have asked me why I didn't leave an abusive boyfriend sooner. All I can say is, it's hard. We have all heard the saying, "Unless you have walked a mile in my shoes, don't judge." I would go further and say, don't judge at all. You cannot really know another person's circumstances.

I grew up on a farm, sheltered from the real world. On the farm, I had everything I needed: family, food, and the comfort of knowing that I was taken care of and protected. My family was loving and I was never around anyone who was abusive. I didn't know what abuse looked like. I didn't really even see that kind of thing on TV. When it started happening to me, I honestly could not see it. It was a time of my life where I was young and naive, and I trusted everyone.

I had very low self-esteem. When I was younger (during elementary and junior high), I was the ugly duckling – with permed hair, ugly glasses, and funky messed-up teeth. I was picked on for being the farm kid, or for being the ugly kid, or for being the weird kid. That took a toll on me. When you don't feel good about yourself, and others are validating that, it gets set in stone for you. When you go down that ugly path, others can see it. They can see your vulnerability and your holes. They see where you are weak, and then they come in and take over.

Maybe you have been there at some time. It may not have been because of your outward appearance, but perhaps it was because you were smart and people called you a nerd, or you were athletic and people labeled you as a jock, or you were just the "odd kid." If you had some kind of label cast upon you, you have had a brush with low self-esteem.

That's probably why I stayed with Eric. Maybe that's why I got into the relationship to begin with. I thought someone cared about me. Someone thought I was pretty enough to be with them. My low self-esteem was further crystallized in my brain when I was repeatedly told that I would never find anyone else to love me if I left.

We don't really realize how things that happened when we were younger have the potential of taking over our lives and making us insecure. I look at how this insecurity has shown itself to me in the entrepreneurial world. I am a person who needs to have approval from others around me; a reassurance that I am doing the right thing and that things will be OK. I used to overcompensate for the insecurities that came from childhood. I was always trying to do more and to achieve more. It was a way of proving to my younger self that I was worthy. And it was a way to prove myself to others who didn't see me as good or as important as I am. And I was telling my past, "Hey, this girl's got it – she can do anything."

I recognize that it's easy to be drawn back into feeling the need for reassurance and approval. When I feel insecurity coming on, I use my core values to bring me back into the present – to know that I no longer need to overcompensate for insecurities. Today, I work hard and achieve from a place of joy and curiosity, instead of a need for approval from others. Rather than constantly trying to prove myself worthy, as I did when I was younger, I honor how I have grown. I don't need others to see me as good or important. When I am living from my core values, I know I can do anything I put my heart and mind to. I feel deep satisfaction within myself.

With age comes wisdom. For years I was hateful; resentful of everything that happened to me. Why was I dealt what I was dealt? The feeling of "Why me?" kicked in. However, over time, something in me changed. I learned that the "weeds" in our lives should not simply be pulled, because we could be pulling other valuable things out with them. My "weeds" were all the bad things that had happened to me; but attached to them were the valuable lessons I learned. There is a great Bible verse that illustrates that point:

Let the weeds and the wheat grow together until the harvest time. At the harvest time I will tell the workers this: First, gather the weeds and tie them together to be burned. Then gather the wheat and bring it to my barn.

Then Jesus told the people another story: God's kingdom is like a mustard seed that a man plants in his field. It is the smallest of all seeds. But when it grows, it is the largest of all garden plants. It becomes a tree big enough for the birds to come and make nests in its branches.

MATTHEW 13:30-32, ERV

I learned to grant myself grace. The dictionary defines grace as to confirm dignity or honor. My definition of grace is to give ourselves a break and to not be so hard on ourselves or others. I learned to think of my past as a learning experience; as a class in life.

I am not sure where I learned about grace or how I even started practicing it. But one day it happened. I started thinking about all the things that "happened" to me in my life and I started seeing them as tools to live. My past has not defined me; I am not the victim. My past has become part of me. My past has become part of my "quilt." In that "quilt," I have woven in the fabric of all of my experiences – good, bad, and ugly. It has become my quilt of life and of **living.** I add to my quilt every day; it is a living and breathing part of me.

When I learned to grant myself grace, my **Inspire** core value came into play. This was a lot of what happened five years ago when I had the crisis that led to me writing and clarifying my core values. I reached a point in my life that I allowed life to **inspire** me.

LIVING WITH GRACE & GRIT
INSPIRE

Hard times and challenges inspired me to reframe things. When life gets tough, use the mantra: everything is **for** me (it is not happening **to** me)! Once I started living by that mantra, things in my life started changing. I changed the way that I would look at situations.

I once had a customer who was very upset about a policy that we had. She did not understand it, and just wanted to let us know how upset she was. She told us that she would not shop at our store again. So, I personally reached out to her and we had a conversation. She could not believe that the owner of the store had called to talk to her. She has been a wonderful customer since then, for almost 10 years.

The lesson I learned? Pick up the phone, talk to the customer and make her feel heard. After all, that is what we all want, 95 percent of the time – to be heard. Changing my lens on any situation so that I see that it's happening **for** me instead of **to** me allowed me to find the good. It is about being empowered, rather than feeling like a victim.

PRACTICE THIS CORE VALUE

When things happen in life, you can choose to become the victim or the victor. Try looking at things that others could see as a problem, challenge or roadblock, and ask yourself:

1. What is the opportunity in this situation?
2. How can I learn from this experience?
3. How can I grow from this challenge?
4. How can I use this situation to help others?
5. What is the best possible outcome of this situation?

We need to embrace change and growth – it's good to get outside your comfort zone. What got you here is not what will get you to the next level. Change allows us the opportunity to grow and become even better. Be excited with change, as with change comes opportunity. Let challenges **inspire** you to be better.

4 Slowing Down to MOVE AHEAD

In our busy lives, we often think that everything has to be done at lightning speed. I certainly know that I feel this way. We constantly check our emails, respond to messages almost immediately, and always have to be reachable. It can seem that if we don't do all those things, we'll fall behind. But what if slowing down is what we need to do, to be able to move forward faster?

We all have times in our lives that slow us down. If you are on a roll working out and then get hurt, that slows you down. In business, kinks happen every day – the order doesn't come in time, the big sale falls through, etc. When you are faced with obstacles, the best thing you can do is to find what I call your "pink space." For me, that "pink space" is all about the most important core value – **Know Yourself**.

Pink space is taking the time to slow down enough to feel all the feelings. It is a pause, like a comma, that allows us to breathe and reflect. Keep in mind that it is a comma, **not** a period. Without pink space in our lives, we are on autopilot; and that does not allow any time for us to reflect or process. When we don't take time to pause, we don't **really** think about things: life, business, family, the future. Pink space has the power to calm us. It anchors us in the present, which reduces our anxiety and helps us see things more clearly. The commas in life allow you to **really** get to know yourself. Then you can rekindle the passion you had to begin with.

When I was on bed rest with my twins, I was also trying to run my wedding and event planning business. However, I was unable to do absolutely anything all day but sit in a chair or lie in bed. It was such a hard thing for me to do. I was young, I was lively, and I was – yes – invincible. And I was frustrated. Looking back, I see how I could have appeared selfish, and that saddens me. If I could have just looked outside myself, to be more selfless, I could have better understood why I was on bed rest. I mean, I understood it, but I wasn't on board with it. It slowed me down, I didn't have control – and I was not happy about it.

I am a doer, but God had other plans during that time. His plan was for me to slow down. I had to learn to calm my mind and find what I would later realize is my **pink space** – so that I would not be anxious, and so that I would allow the world to happen around me while I was protecting my babies. Unfortunately, the **pink space** did not reveal itself to me during my time of bed rest. I really wish I had known about that concept back then, because it would have really helped me. I would not learn about it until many years later.

By nature, I am a fast-moving vehicle. It took me a while, but I realized that about myself. I tell people that God made me short because I go fast and low to the ground. I zip everywhere. That's my nature. I like to be doing many different tasks and juggling many different things. I multitask like it's my job. That is OK to a point; however, I had to learn the art of slowing down.

I often have to step away from whatever it is I am doing and look at what surrounds me. I know myself better now, so I know that I need to make the time to take it all in… and be still. I certainly can't take it all in when I am running from here to there to everywhere, and being everything to everyone!

I have learned in my business life that if I'm able to just take a step, and then take another step, and then take another step – with time in between to reflect on what has just happened or what's about to happen **(pink space)** – I'm a much more effective leader. I'm also a much more effective friend, and a more compassionate person. In this

pink space, I learned who I was. It was where I learned what makes me "tick" as a person. I was able to define my wants, needs and desires.

Again, if we're moving too quickly, we don't have the ability to figure out what just happened and dissect it. We're not able to take whatever is happening for us at that moment and do something good with it. The small amount of **pink space** is vitally important.

LIVING WITH GRACE & GRIT
KNOW YOURSELF

Get to **Know Yourself.** What makes you excited, happy, frustrated? In business, knowing yourself is critical. I was once dealing with a customer who wanted to return something; she was adamant. I explained how our return policy worked, but nothing that I said made her understand. I was unable to reason with her. It was as though she knew what my hot buttons were, and she kept pressing them. Before I knew myself, I would have been frustrated and upset, and I would have taken her behavior personally. However, once I really came to know myself, I could identify my triggers before I became frustrated. Being able to do that helped me get through that tough situation and allowed me to help the customer.

Find your pink space and reflect on who you are. There is a lot of beauty in slowing down and taking in all that surrounds us. It also allows our mind to calm down and just be present. We can just sit where we are at the moment. Life is fast, and we make it go even faster when we always have to be on the run and movin' and shakin'. Take that time in your pink space and just... be.

PRACTICE THIS CORE VALUE

I know that it's very hard to slow down. But we must do it. Once we start looking at slowing down as a positive, we will see the great value that has been given to us, along with a precious, precious resource called time. Slowing down is one of the fundamental factors in our long-term success, because it allows you to make decisions based on facts rather than just emotions. That precious time that is between an action and your response is very critical to your overall success. Once you know who you are, navigating the world and those around you will be easier.

Questions to ask:

1. What is it that I am rushing for? Why is it important for me to get to the "finish line" of what it is that I am doing?

2. What can I take off my plate today that will allow me to live for the moment? (Maybe instead of always saying "yes," say "no" or "maybe.")
3. What are the small things that I can do right now to be present? (Perhaps focus on your breathing, or your thoughts?)
4. What am I missing out on by not being able to be in the present? (More often than not, if we change the reference to "what am I missing out on," FOMO hits and we pay closer attention.)
5. What would it look like if I slowed down? Is the world going to end? Is my company going to collapse because I am not moving as fast? (The answer is almost always no!)

5 Let Go of WHAT YOU KNOW

Have you ever found yourself clinging to something that you know is no longer serving you? Maybe it was a toxic relationship, a dead-end job, or a negative belief about yourself.

Letting go can be one of the hardest things we ever do. It's normal to want to hold on to things that are familiar, even if they're causing us pain. But sometimes, the only way to move forward is to let go of the past. Letting go is not forgetting about the past, or pretending it didn't happen; it is about accepting it and moving on.

By 2009, when the twins were 2 ½ years old, my husband Brad started a business in Florida and he was traveling back and forth. He would be gone for a week or two at a time, and I was at home alone with the twins. It was challenging to run two businesses in two different states, especially with two toddlers. So, we made the difficult decision to move from Minnesota, the only state that we had ever known, to Florida – a state where we knew no one.

We moved during the housing crisis of 2009. We tried to sell the wedding and event planning business and the bridal shop, but we were unsuccessful. So I ran the business in absentia with a manager in place until we were able to sell, a year and a half later.

That year and a half was traumatic for me. I didn't want to move to Florida. I didn't want to leave my family. I didn't want to leave my business. Yet, I knew in my brain that it was the best thing for Brad and me and the twins, because Florida was where my husband's business was. However, my heart was hurting because I had created something from nothing, and now, I had to give it all up.

After all I had been through, I had a desire to be an equal with my husband professionally. The idea excited me and filled me up. Even though my husband already saw me as an equal, I did not see it that way. I felt so hurt and resentful; the pain was so deep. The business that I had created was my validation that I was OK – that I was worthy and that I mattered. I think that is why I tried to hold on so tightly to Heartstrings Bridal – because it was a symbol for me. It was a symbol of the new me; it was a symbol of freedom. My business was part of me. It represented the validation that I had been searching for since I was a young girl. When we finally sold the business, I still had some resentment. I felt as though I had given up a part of myself with that business.

As entrepreneurs we allow our businesses to become part of us. The business becomes part of our identity. When we no longer have that identity, we go through a grieving process. Again, I think I was holding on so tightly because that business was **me;** that was my identity, and that was what validated my whole being. There I was, married to an amazing man, with beautiful children that we had waited for and had worked so hard to keep alive, and yet my identity was as a business owner.

I don't remember the exact moment that I finally was able to let go and move on without feeling that hurt or that resentment. Still, I honestly think that it was another moment of fate for me. Without letting go, I don't think I could have gone through all that I did on my own and come out on the other side of it as whole, as fulfilled, and as peaceful as I did.

I will be honest. Getting over being resentful was not an "overnight success." However, core values overlap and work together. I drew on **faith** to get through. I also came to **know myself** better. And I learned how to **be humble** as I **let go.** With values, it is not always clear-cut; values will most certainly overlap in most situations. My values always do. Each value that I hold is intertwined with the others, and it's nearly impossible to have one without another. For example, my core values of **"make it happen"** and **"own it"** go hand in hand, as do **"have faith"** and **"inspire."**

Holding on can stop the flow of the life we are meant to live. Once I let go of the business and all the intense emotions that went along with it, I allowed other wonderful things to flow into my life. Creating space does that. Because I let go of the negative, it allowed us to meet some of our very best friends, and we started another business.

Many people look at letting go as something negative, but I learned to look at it this way: by letting something in my life go I am opening the door for something even more wonderful. Again, it was not easy and it didn't happen for me overnight. As a matter of fact, there are still times that I have to wake myself up and say, "Hey, remember, this letting go may not be a bad thing." I have allowed myself to be humble, and I let go of my ego and agenda because they were in the way of my happiness. Along the way, I also learned to not blame others. Those lessons were all part of my journey to **be humble!** This is how this core value of **Be Humble** revealed itself to me.

CHAPTER 5

LIVING WITH GRACE & GRIT

BE HUMBLE

Life can be filled with bumps, bruises, heartbreak. However, it can also be filled with joy, love, laughter – and a whole lot of fun. We need to allow ourselves to let go of the things that may not be serving us to make room for those things that come into our lives to make us better; to make us whole. I know it is not an easy thing to do, and you will find that with everything life throws at you, you may need to check yourself every now and again. But that's OK. A good friend of mine had a saying, "*Po' body is nerfect,*" which means "Nobody is perfect." I think back to that saying every time something does not go quite right.

PRACTICE THIS CORE VALUE

Think of things in your life that may be holding you back. It may be something that happened today, or something from years ago. Is there still resentment that you have about it, and are you allowing your pride to get in the way? Remember, there is no room for ego. Let that thought help guide you toward being humble.

Key questions you can ask yourself to determine if you are humble, or if you need more humble pie in your life:

1. How do I respond when I am criticized? Do I become defensive and angry?
2. How do I respond when I am wrong? Do I have a hard time asking for help or apologizing?
3. Do I see good in others? Am I quick to judge or criticize?
4. Am I willing to serve others? Am I more willing to be served or to serve?
5. How do I handle successes and failures? Do I allow success to go to my head, or do I learn from it and move on?

6 Rise Above
BETRAYAL

Betrayal. It can leave an indelible mark on our lives. It's a violation of trust, a breach of loyalty, a wound that cuts deep into our sense of security and self-worth. It shakes our foundation. Yet, despite the pain it inflicts, betrayal can also be a catalyst for growth; a crucible that can shape our resilience and mold our perspectives.

It happens to the best of us. We choose trusted business partners, friends, employees – and then they drive by and give us the middle finger, so to speak. They betray or sabotage us in some way. Betrayal is a painful experience, and it can leave us feeling hurt, angry, and confused. It can be difficult to know how to move on from betrayal, but it is possible to rise above it – and even become stronger. Our core values can help us in betrayal situations, and betrayal can lead us to uncover our values as well. As with many of my life experiences, betrayal helped me to clarify a core value.

I had a dream of owning a clothing store. However, everything I was doing as an entrepreneur seemed to take me further away from that. I was fond of consignment stores and garage sales. After all, I have always had fond memories of going to garage sales with my grandmother while I was growing up. Finally, after moving to Florida, I took a leap of faith and started True Fashionistas, a lifestyle resale store for women, men, and the home. It was a way to pay homage to my fond memories of growing up and enjoying those garage sale moments with my grandmother. It also allowed me to fulfill my dream of owning a clothing store.

When I started True Fashionistas, I didn't really have the money to start it, because I still owned a business in Minnesota and was waiting for it to sell. I had the knowledge to start a business, but not the money. But a trusted friend was willing to provide the money and we would be 50-50 partners. We got along great; we picked the decor for the entire store, we opened it, and we enjoyed running it together.

However, a few months into the business, she decided she didn't want to do business with me anymore. Brad and I were left with a choice to either buy her out or give her the business. We chose to buy her out. The very next day, she signed a lease on a store space a few doors down from mine – and it was the exact same type of business. To top it off, she took all my employees, except for one.

Yes, that one stung and it stung badly. I mean, imagine being bitten by a mosquito, bee and alligator all at the same time, while also being kicked in the stomach and then being run over by a slow-moving vehicle. Yeah… it hurt that badly. Up until that point, it had never occurred to me that another human being could do something like that in business. I had been mistreated by my high school boyfriend; however, this was the business world. Wasn't everyone supposed to be nice and kind and ethical to each other in business? I couldn't wrap my head around it. I could not figure out what went wrong.

But it didn't really matter. I had to move on. I remember calling a very trusted confidant to come down and talk with me about what had happened, and she said, "Jennifer, everything is going to be just fine, and you are going to totally kick ***."

I was still looking for validation from outside! There it was, rearing its ugly head again. I needed someone from outside my head to validate that everything was going to be OK. I needed to be told: "You are going to get through this, and you're going to come out the other side stronger than ever."

While the situation was happening, it took me back to the days when my twins were born, and the doctors had said to us, "Everything is going to be OK. They are going to grow up and be strong, healthy children and teenagers and young adults." Sadly, I didn't believe them then. I couldn't see what was in front of me to believe that was possible. Now, my children have graduated high school and are in college, so I can testify that **yes, everything will be OK!** Everything will all work out in the manner that God has intended.

As it turned out, everything truly was OK; and it was going to get even better. Taking over the business allowed me to begin working alongside my husband. We would find out that he is better than I am at handling many parts of the business; and we would discover that I excel at things that he doesn't. We make a good team.

Even though the business betrayal was a horrible thing for me to go through, I kept my cool and took the high road. Sure, I could have slandered my former partner's new business. I could have slashed her tires… but I didn't. Someone once told me, "Don't let someone live rent-free in your head." That is good advice. When we are faced with a situation where someone has done us wrong, taking the high road is always the best option. We do not want to give away our power. Do the right thing, and everything will turn out OK… it's called **karma.**

LIVING WITH GRACE & GRIT
CREATE HONEST RELATIONSHIPS

From that business experience, I learned the power of **creating honest relationships.** From there on out, I was only going to surround myself with people who were honest and authentic. I realized that the kind of betrayal I experienced is very much a loss (like a death in a way). There are steps that I walked through to work through the process:

1. **Feel the emotions.** I allowed myself to feel the emotions (which is very healthy). I let it all out; I expressed my feelings. I allowed myself to cry, scream, and be angry. I did not bottle my feelings up or pretend everything was OK, but rather I acknowledged and processed emotions.
2. **Don't blame yourself.** I am not proud to say that I blamed myself. It is easy to fall into the trap of blaming yourself for the actions of others. In hindsight, I realize I was not responsible for the actions of the person who decided to betray me. She is the one who made the decision.

3. **Practice self-care.** Talking to trusted friends, family, or even a therapist is very helpful. Our support system is everything. They help us navigate our feelings.
4. **Don't rush into anything**. Don't make rash decisions after a betrayal. I think of it like avoiding a rebound relationship. We don't want to step into something just because someone betrayed us or let us down (or ended our relationship). I gave myself time to heal and figure out what was next. By doing that, we can go into whatever is next with a clear mind.
5. **Forgive yourself and others**. It is easier said than done. "Forgive" does not mean "forget"; it just means letting go of anger and resentment. Those feelings are toxic. Once I let go of the negative feelings, I was free, and that freedom allowed bigger and better things to enter my life.
6. **Learn from the situation.** Betrayal can be painful and hard to understand. If we take time to reflect on what happened, we can learn from it, and the experience will help us avoid betrayal in the future.

PRACTICE THIS CORE VALUE

Always Do The Right Thing. Always keep yourself in check.

Questions to help you practice this core value:

1. Am I taking the high road when someone says or does something nasty to me?
2. Am I retorting back to them with angry, nasty words if they dish them out to me?
3. Am I willing to give someone a second chance after they did something wrong?
4. Am I willing to be vulnerable with others and share my authentic self?
5. Am I a good listener? Am I able to listen to others without judgment or interruption?

7 Chose Your COMPANY WISELY

*H*ave you ever considered the impact that the people you surround yourself with have on your life? The individuals you choose to spend your time and energy with can either elevate you toward your aspirations or weigh you down, hindering your progress and dimming your inner light. The concept was something that had occurred to me years ago – but I didn't really **think** about it.

As the betrayal by my business partner shows, the company that we keep is so very important. But before we know who that company should be, we have to know what we stand for. We must know what our core values are, so that we know who will align with who we are and who we want to be.

In high school when I was with the abusive boyfriend, I didn't know what I stood for. I didn't know who I was; and therefore, I attracted the wrong people into my life. Have you had that kind of experience? We should all listen to our "gut feeling" when we meet someone. That first initial thought that goes through our head is not a judgment, it's a feeling. People have different energies, and only some will be a match for us.

There was a time in one of my businesses where I was involved with some people who didn't necessarily align with my beliefs and values. Finally, there was a major event that allowed me to step back and see what was really happening. I was in the trenches, working on the problem, and I couldn't see what was happening. However, when the event occurred, I was able to see those around me for who they really were.

The catastrophic event was COVID-19. It brought me to a different place in life. I came to realize that I needed to learn how to have some hard conversations. Ultimately, facing such a challenge would grow me as a person and it would also grow me as an entrepreneur. No, it wasn't pleasant, it was not fun, but it was a necessity. I had to take myself to the next level and move forward. This is something we are always doing as entrepreneurs. There is always a growing edge as we evolve and improve in our quest for success. To evolve, we must remember that what got us here will not always be enough to get us where we want to go.

I realized that certain individuals didn't align with me or with my brand. That realization allowed me to step back and see that I needed to change some things and surround myself with people who are positive, caring and understanding. I needed people around me who would align with what I believed and with my core values – people that cared about me and my business.

I still initially assume positive intent when meeting and interacting with people, but I trust my intuition and use my other core values to guide me as well.

It was a very hard time in my life. I am not someone who can let go of relationships easily, and I do not like conflict. My past has made me a person who doesn't like conflict and who doesn't like having hard conversations. It is my nature to assume the best motives in others. In the situation during COVID, my core value that assumes positive intent actually took me to an uncomfortable spot. Most of the time, my core values guide me to the right spot; but in this case, it took me to a place of clouded judgment. I misjudged the character of others.

I have now surrounded myself with an "A-team" of people who are aligned with my values and understand what I stand for. It has made all of the difference. It has allowed me to let go of feeling that I had to do every task myself; now, I delegate responsibility. I trust my employees to lead my business in the direction that follows my core values. They have the best intentions for the company as well.

In fact, my team understands my core values so well that when we relocated our store and I was unable to help them move (I had surgery), they moved the contents of two stores into one huge store… in one day! Yes, all in one day – on a Sunday, when we were closed. My team started working at 6 a.m. and did not stop until midnight! And they did not let me lift a finger. Why? Because they were aligned with my core values. They went the extra mile, and were willing to do what it took to accomplish the job. They knew I could not do it – and they did it **for** me!

COVID taught me how important it is to let go of people who are not serving you. When they don't support you, your vision, or your values, they should not be in your life. Even more, they should not be in your business – because business is much less forgiving to misalignment than our personal lives are.

When I started surrounding myself with people who lined up with my core values, I saw a huge shift in my business – and in me, personally. I became a much more confident person, who was more empathetic and more understanding. I could see the bigger picture and I no longer acted out of fear. Being led by fear is no way to live life.

I learned to follow my gut, but also to **Assume Positive Intent**.

LIVING WITH GRACE & GRIT
ASSUME POSITIVE INTENT

Surround yourself with the right people – those who serve you. Those who make you feel good, and those who allow others to feel good. There have been times in my life that I have hired people for my businesses who didn't align with me and didn't align with my business. That caused almost insurmountable amounts of stress in my life and made me feel miserable. It was only when I realized that, and moved on and hired people who actually did align with me and my business, that I was able to change the entire trajectory of my business and my life. I knew that my new employees aligned with me because they made decisions in a way that was consistent with my values. They treated everyone with respect. They not only supported my goals and ambitions, but those of the company as well. However, the most important thing was that I felt that I could be myself around them. All I had to do was ask the right questions. Aligning with the right people allowed me to delegate more, rely on others more, and most importantly – **trust more.**

PRACTICE THIS CORE VALUE

Questions you can ask yourself about assuming positive intent:

1. What assumptions am I making about the other person's intent?
2. What risks do I take if I assume negative intent?
3. What benefits am I likely to experience if I assume positive intent?
4. What is the most generous explanation for the other person's behavior?
5. Is there any evidence to support my assumption?
6. What do they bring to my life?
7. Do they bring positive vibes? Or negative?
8. How does my gut feel when I am with them?

These are simple questions you can ask yourself and do that "gut check." Remember, our core values will rarely lead us down the wrong path.

8 Grow From Survival TO SUCCESS

In life and in business, I am sure that we have all experienced moments when we feel like we are merely surviving; just treading water. We may feel stuck, overwhelmed, and unsure of our path forward. But amid such struggles lies the potential for growth, waiting to be unleashed. The journey from survival to success is not a linear path; it's a winding road, filled with twists, turns, and unexpected detours.

But with unwavering determination, a growth mindset, and a supportive community, we can transform our challenges into stepping stones, our doubts into motivation, and our fears into fuel for our dreams.

The business that Brad had started in 2009 came to a crashing end in 2014 when the State of Florida shut down all the businesses in the industry overnight. Some businesses in the industry were not doing things according to the law. Even though my husband's business had crossed all their t's and dotted their i's, it paid the same price. You know the saying – a few bad apples spoil the bunch.

Up until that point, my husband had been the breadwinner in the family. And while I really appreciated him in that role, I wanted to be an equal to him – because, after all, weren't we in this thing called life together? So, when the new laws ended my husband's business, all that went through my thoughts – and through his mind as well – was, *Now,* ***we*** *have to do this* **together.** *We have to continue to grow True Fashionistas and make that our focus.*

Now was our moment – we were setting ourselves up to be that husband-and-wife team that conquered the business world; the resale business world, anyway.

I don't remember much about the days between when his business had to close and the years after. I just remember the "freak out" moments that I had. I was afraid we would lose everything and end up with nothing, after all that hard work and moving to Florida! I was not only nervous; I was mad. I went into survival mode. I learned a valuable lesson. Ask for what you want; however, you must be prepared to receive it. Yes, be prepared to receive it.

Together, Brad and I made a goal to take our business to the next level. That is when I discovered my core value of **Make It Happen**. We both took personal responsibility for making things happen; we hit the ground running, every day. We put our heads down and worked hard – harder than I think we had ever worked in our life. I would get to work at 5:30 a.m. and come home at 7 p.m. Brad would make dinner for us; we would help the kids with homework, and I would do some housework. Then, as soon as we put the kids to bed, Brad and I would sit down and work some more. My husband was there right alongside me.

Brad was, and still is, so instrumental in making our personal and professional lives work. He is financially skilled in a way that I am not. He takes care of things on the back side of the business, and I take care of the customer and the front side of the business. I would go to the store at crazy hours of the early morning to do everything there, and he would get the kids ready and take them to school. We were a true partnership. We were in it together, and it felt good to have someone as a partner in life and in business that has your back. It was tiring, but we were both working toward a common goal – to grow and build our business and provide for our family. It also allowed us to get closer as a couple, which was the wonderful unexpected outcome of the entire situation.

Rinse and repeat, day in and day out, for months and years on end. It was emotionally and physically exhausting. I wore that exhaustion like a badge, which is not a good thing. However, it is what I thought I had to do at the time to make sure our family was OK. My idea was: The more we worked, the better we could provide for our family. Little did I know that I was also shielding myself from any pain, hurt, and what might feel like defeat. I was running from my emotions by working and working and working, **all** of the time. I was also acting out of fear of losing everything; yet, that fear is what pushed me forward and allowed me to become so persistent.

I had to convince myself that it was going to work. It simply had to. There was no other option.

As humans, when we are confronted with what we perceive as "impossible," our faith is what guides us through. Our faith leads us down the path that we need to follow. So, Make It Happen is a powerful core value. But we have to temper it with the others. We just have to be sure to allow ourselves some grace, and we need to get out of our own way, so we can step into that pink space. We need to be quiet enough to allow it all to work. We need to allow ourselves the time to be quiet enough to listen.

CHAPTER 8

LIVING WITH GRACE *&* GRIT
MAKE IT HAPPEN

Remember, we all have a path; a journey we are supposed to be on. I allowed it to happen; I fought for it, too, and I owned it. I took responsibility for making things happen. After my husband's business closed, I stepped up. I did not make excuses but looked at ways that I could make something happen. The True Fashionista journey was one where I moved from survival to success. I started it to survive, but it became a thriving, successful business! Success, however, can bring challenges, and can sometimes lead us away from our values and our guidance system.

I knew that True Fashionistas was a success when we were approached by one of the largest mall owners in the country, asking if we wanted to be in their mall. For me, it was as if George Clooney had come over and given me a big smooch on my lips (you can insert whoever your "it" person of the moment is)! I was **so** excited. I thought, *They are asking us! Oh my gosh, they want us to be at their center.*

It was like I'd won an Emmy. How could we pass up that opportunity? We just had to do it. I convinced myself, and then my husband (he is the cautious one of the two of us), that we had to move on it! We had to act immediately,

I felt, or they would find someone else. There were *whispers* in the background, but the voice of excitement was too loud for me to hear them.

We had made it to the big time! At the mall, we had our entire space built out. Then, the day before we were to move in, the mall company came to us and said, "We've got a problem. There are three stores that do not want you in our center. So, you have two options – either leave and pretend none of this ever happened, or move in and not carry the brands carried by the three stores." The brands in question were some of our largest-selling brands.

So, we struck a deal with the mall to move in on a 30-day trial. If it wasn't working for us after that time, we could break the contract. We were out of their center within nine months.

If only I had listened to the whispers, I would have saved us a lot of money and heartache. But I let my ego get in the way and made a decision that I would not have made if I had been still enough to hear the whispers. Remember to always come back to your core values and to listen to your guidance system!

PRACTICE THIS CORE VALUE

Look at your life. Are there areas where you say to yourself, "I can't do that," or "I don't know how." Then, figure it out! Like author-entrepreneur Marie Forleo says, "Everything is figureoutable."

Are there spots in your life that are holding you back? Perhaps it is the fear of not succeeding, or of not having enough money. There are many excuses that we can make. Identify those areas of fear and find what is holding you back; then, take over the narrative, take the reins, and make it happen.

Consider these questions:

1. Whatever it is that is holding me back, is it real or is it in my head?
2. What is the fear that is holding me back?
3. What is the payoff for staying stuck?
4. What are the consequences of staying stuck?
5. What is something I can do to move one step closer to my goal?

9 *Role* REVERSAL

*L*ife is full of unexpected turns, twists, and detours. They can send us on journeys we do not anticipate. For many women, the path of becoming an equal with their spouse may not have been part of their initial plans. However, life has a way of challenging our expectations and pushing us beyond our perceived limitations.

I had thought that being an equal with my husband would come with the validation that I was "somebody"; that I was doing something right. I had imagined that the world would care and that I would be put up on a pedestal. But being equal with him and sharing responsibility – not just at home, but also at work – brought challenges that I was not even aware of right away.

I went from being a **mom with a business** to a **business owner** with my husband. I found myself at the forefront of everything that we did. I became the company spokesperson, mascot, and most definitely the company's doer of everything... except for the financials. As I said before, my husband is the one who is more financially skilled in this family. I was most certainly a "yes girl." I said "yes" to any work that I thought needed to be done. I thought that being a "yes girl" would give me that financial freedom I was so yearning for. Somehow, I thought that if I put in the physical labor that it would equal more money for my business, and in turn, my family. **Wrong.** That is not how it works.

In fact, I have now learned – with my years of wisdom – that by saying yes to work at the business, I was saying no to something else. That something else was time with my family. I was always working. I was not really with my family during that time, even though we were together. My mind was everywhere else instead of where I was. I was always thinking of the next thing I had to do. I was in the store, working all of the time; I was doing the labor that needed to be done, day in and day out. I would learn the hard way that some lessons have to be learned by living them.

My constant working also brought about an interesting shift between me and my husband. The entire time we were dating, and even when we first got married, he would work all day. After work, he just wanted to come home, because he was so exhausted. I, on the other hand, would love to go out and have fun. Not to a party – because I don't drink, never have, and probably never will. I just wanted to go out to dinner, movies, golf and hang out with friends.

When our business began to my full attention, my husband and I naturally switched roles. He became more social after work, because he was in the office behind a desk all day. In contrast, I craved solitude upon returning home, usually retreating into my pajamas, a laptop, a notebook, or a book in front of the TV. (I have always been a multitasker. I usually feel the need to have something to occupy my mind while watching TV. Perhaps it's a lingering sense of guilt about indulging in downtime.)

I discovered why the role switch happened. Remember, I was the one who faced the customers each day. Brad was behind a computer screen. I had my fill of social "beeness" during the day with customers, but he needed a way to have his social time outside of work. (I get it now!)

I took my core value of **Make It Happen** to exhaustion. I was willing to do whatever it took to accomplish the job (which provided financial stability for my family) and just a little more. Somehow, I thought that working all those hours would be the "cherry on the top"!

It has taken me years, and lots and lots of practice, to come to the realization that I had to learn to delegate the right things to the right people. That way, I was not doing it all myself; yet, I was still able to honor my **Make It Happen** core value. We have all heard the saying, "Work smarter, not harder." But I had done the opposite – I worked harder and not smarter.

When my twins entered their junior year in high school, I realized that if I was truly surrounding myself with great people that cared, I could delegate. I could entrust tasks to them that I was not the best at – or the most efficient at – and all would be well. When I discovered that, I was a changed woman! I discovered my core value of **Own It.** I would need to own what worked, and what did not. I saw that I would have to **own** the areas where I was not working smart.

LIVING WITH GRACE & GRIT
OWN IT

The grass is not always greener on the other side of the fence. I am happy, thankful and grateful for what I have. I definitely didn't start here; I had to learn to take time to find what makes me happy, thankful and grateful. Today, I intentionally remind myself what those things are, and focus on bringing them into my life as often as possible.

You don't have to do it all yourself. Leverage what you are good at, and surround yourself with those who can help you in the areas where you need help. Knowing that I can do that is what allows me to go that extra mile in my business, and in my daily interaction with others.

Find the areas in your business that are your strong points, and also the ones you are not so good at or take too long to do. Hire those tasks out. Stick with the things that you are passionate about and really enjoy. Doing that will not only fill your heart, but also will ensure that you have less possibility of burnout.

PRACTICE THIS CORE VALUE

Where in your life or your business are the areas where you are not so great?

Make that list; it all starts with a list. Then ask these questions:

1. For which items or areas can I hire someone to help me?
2. Are there any of those items that I can simply remove?
3. What areas of my business do I dread, or avoid, or procrastinate on?
4. In what area of my business am I least skilled?
5. What area of my business am I not delegating effectively?

10 Unfinished BUSINESS

While writing this book, I had a lot of trepidation and was worried about what other people would think. *Will they think I am weak? Will they think less of me?* Then, I came to a realization. Just as my story of abuse had motivated others, my story of how I succeeded in my life and my business could also perhaps be a catalyst for someone else. My experience might inspire them to look at their personal or their professional life, and encourage them to question things. My journey could possibly move them to grow and discover their passions, strengths, and true being.

As I look back at my life, I see all the times that I had to sacrifice. There were times when life was downright tough. I could have felt sorry for myself or felt like a victim. But I realized that that was a waste of time; precious time. Instead, I saw that I could be doing something worthwhile for myself and those around me – whether they were family, friends, or strangers.

Sacrifice is a part of life. We must sacrifice to achieve anything. The magic is in finding the balance – between yourself, work, family, friends, business and community. I spent many years looking toward the end result, but I have realized that the middle is where we need to live. **Now** matters as much as the end. Now, in the present, is where I discover my core value of **Laugh and Have Fun.** This value balances all of the others.

So now, in every moment I get with my family, I try to be present. Life is really meant to be lived in the moment. Time is the only thing we can't get more of. I am not perfect. I have to allow myself grace; I am human. Yes, sometimes I pick up my phone to check my messages. However, my children are quick to remind me to get off my phone, even if they get on theirs one second after telling me.

Since my core values have become clear to me, and because I now live them in every area of my life, I feel empowered. I am able to do wonderful things that bring me much of what I have been looking for. I even ended up going back to college to finish my four-year degree. I went back to school for **me.** I had always wanted to do it, and finally, I just went for it.

I started another company, mentoring and coaching women who are small-business owners. I use everything I have learned to help them. I started speaking to audiences to share the knowledge, wisdom and experience I have gained in business and in life. When I speak, I weave in my story of challenge and success, in the hope that I will help someone. I stand in my truth and share my strength and voice, along with my core values, with others who may not have found their power yet. I have also created space to be involved in local civic life and in nonprofit organizations. I think it's important for me to give back to my community.

LIVING WITH GRACE & GRIT
LAUGH AND HAVE FUN

Appreciate the journey. Life is not always going to go the way we want it to, or the way we expect it to. There will be bumps, hairpin turns, and deep potholes. We trudge through them or detour around them, and come out on the other side stronger than ever. But with all the challenges, it's still important to remember to Laugh and Have Fun. It is such a valuable value to have, especially at work.

At True Fashionistas, we believe in having fun and laughing every day. We have all kinds of parties and contests. In fact, every Halloween, we have a costume contest;

the entire staff dresses up and the winner gets awards. It is so much fun and such a great team-building activity.

PRACTICE THIS CORE VALUE

Are you all business and no play? Here are five questions you can ask yourself:

1. How often do I laugh on a daily basis?
2. Do I have things in my life that I look forward to?
3. Do I have enough time for leisure activities that I enjoy?
4. Am I surrounded by people who make me laugh and have fun?
5. Do I feel happy and fulfilled with my life?

Have fun. Don't take things so personally. Laugh every day. Work hard, but remember to balance your time among work, family, friends and community. Life is too short to not be the best person you can be. And, you get what you give. Live in the present.

CONCLUSION

Looking Back and MOVING AHEAD

Life and business are like a journey. Along the way, we discover and rediscover our core values. My journey as an entrepreneur was no different; each core value that I hold today has come from circumstances that were in God's hands. He handed them to me, and I made them my own. Here they are again:

1. Have Faith
2. Inspire
3. Know Yourself
4. Be Humble
5. Create Honest Relationships
6. Assume Positive Intent
7. Make It Happen
8. Own It
9. Laugh and Have Fun

It was through living every day that these core values were revealed to me. But be aware that your values will not reveal themselves to you in a bright pink neon sign. They will speak to you in *whispers* (that you might not hear for a while). It was only when I went through the storm, and came out on the other side, that I realized the value in the journey. Each core value that I hold today has come from circumstances that were in God's hands. He handed them to me and I made them my own.

Core values can change; they are fluid. You will constantly be adding to – or refining – your core values, and perhaps removing one if it no longer serves you. The most important thing to remember in your life is to Know Yourself. One way to do this is to Be Still and you will find your core values. For me, that is in my pink space. We all need to allow ourselves, and those around us, the grace to sit quietly and observe what is happening around us. If we do this simple, yet hard task, it can help calm our mind and soothe our body. We can prepare. This quiet preparation helps us to find clarity, so that we can make decisions and move forward. And when your cup is empty, fill it up with things that matter: friends, family, relationships.

Your scars are a reminder that you have been through something difficult, and have come out stronger. Find the beauty in your scars. Remember to have the Grace to forgive yourself and others, and the Grit to not give up, no matter how hard things get.

Acknowledgments

I am incredibly grateful to the many people who helped me write this book.

First and foremost, I would like to thank Brad, Brady, and Gracie, and all of my family and friends for their love and encouragement throughout the writing process. I am so grateful for your patience and understanding.

I am also grateful to April and Heather for their expertise and guidance. They helped me shape this book into the best version it could be.

Finally, to my readers: Thank you for choosing to read my book. I hope that it can offer inspiration, knowledge, and the tools you need to be able to find your core values.

I hope that this book helps aspiring entrepreneurs everywhere to overcome their self-doubt and build the confidence they need to succeed.

APPENDIX

The Grace & Grit
TOOLKIT

RESOURCES FOR ENTREPRENEURS

CORE VALUE CHALLENGE

94

JENNIFER'S CORE VALUES

99

GRACE & GRIT

CORE VALUE CHALLENGE

Questions to Ask Yourself to Find Your Core Values

CONSIDER	SHARE YOUR THOUGHTS
What do you enjoy celebrating?	
What frustrates you?	

CORE VALUE CHALLENGE

What do you want more of?

What do you want less of?

What do you want to be known for?

What are your top three successes?

1.

2.

3.

What are your three biggest failures?

1) _____

2) _____

3) _____

What are your strengths? What do other people say when you ask them about your strengths?

What are your weaknesses? What do other people say when you ask them about your weaknesses?

JENNIFER'S CORE VALUES

These are the core values that guide me in both my business and personal life. I have created a deep dive into each here for you so that you can further clarify your own core values. I encourage you to reflect on your own values and write them down until they feel right.

1. **HAVE FAITH**
2. **INSPIRE**
3. **KNOW YOURSELF**
4. **BE HUMBLE**
5. **CREATE HONEST RELATIONSHIPS**
6. **ASSUME POSITIVE INTENT**
7. **MAKE IT HAPPEN**
8. **OWN IT**
9. **LAUGH AND HAVE FUN**

1) HAVE FAITH

- Have belief in a higher power.

2) INSPIRE

- Be positive – you are the company that you keep. In all things, there is goodness.
- Welcome change. What brought you here only works for so long. Growth allows us to become even better. Be excited because change brings opportunities.
- When you see someone doing something fabulous, acknowledge it and cheer them on.

3) KNOW YOURSELF

- Of all the core values, this is the most important one. Know yourself, know your power, take action, and care for each other, your customers and yourself.

4) BE HUMBLE

- Be open to positive and constructive feedback.
- Don't ask your team to do things you would not do yourself.
- There is no room for ego. Don't allow your ego to get in the way of doing what is best for the team.
- Don't blame others. Ask, "What can I do to make this better?" with every mistake.

5. CREATE HONEST RELATIONSHIPS

- Always do the right thing even when others are not watching. Always tell the truth. Be impeccable with your words.
- Always speak the truth with respect and keep your promises.
- Trust, but verify. Assume the best-case scenario or truth, but verify the information.

6. ASSUME POSITIVE INTENT

- Listen twice as much as you talk. (God gave you two ears and only one mouth for a reason.) Be present in the moment. Listen to understand.
- Instead of jumping to conclusions or assuming the worst, embrace curiosity. Gather information, ask questions, and believe that most people act with good intentions (until you see otherwise).
- Be a good team member. Be willing to help and collaborate.
- Make a difference. Always smile and say, "Hi" – it may change someone's day, or even their life.
- Get involved in your community, doing good for others can make a difference.

7 MAKE IT HAPPEN

- Go the extra mile. Do what it takes to accomplish a job – and then do just a little more. It will grow you and teach you every step of the way. I love the book *The Power of One More* by Ed Mylett for this very reason.
- Always be learning new things. Learning will expand your job and your life.
- **Fabulous** customer service begins with **you.** Create customer loyalty by going above and beyond, and by doing the unexpected. Underpromise and overdeliver.

8 OWN IT

- Use good judgment. If your gut tells you something is NOT a good idea, it is probably not. Stop and breathe before speaking or making a decision.
- Embrace ownership. Let your actions, not excuses, define your journey.
- Lead by example. Do unto others as you would have them do unto you. Be a friend to others as the friend you would like to have.
- Take pride in all that you do.

9. LAUGH AND HAVE FUN

- Don't take things personally.
- Take time to laugh every day.
- Work hard but remember family, friends, and loved ones are the cornerstones of our happiness. Make time for them, cherish their presence, and invest in nurturing these precious relationships. Remember, the greatest rewards in life often come from the heart, not the paycheck.

About the AUTHOR

Jennifer Johnson is an entrepreneur, businesswoman, model, and actress. She grew up on a farm in rural Minnesota, where she learned her unwavering work ethic. She is a former Ms. Petite Minnesota.

Starting her career in the bridal industry, Jennifer owned and operated a successful, nationally-recognized wedding and event planning business. She was featured on shows such as *Inside Edition, Home Delivery,* and several local TV and radio programs as a wedding professional.

She and her husband, Brad, are the founders of True Fashionistas, the largest luxury lifestyle resale store in the state of Florida. Her dream was to bring designer clothing, accessories, home decor, and great customer service to others at great prices. Jennifer is also the founder and owner of three other businesses: The Confident Entrepreneur, Pink Farmhouse and Cooies Cookies.

A graduate of the Leadership Collier Class of 2023 and the SBA (Small Business Association) Emerging Leaders Program, Jennifer's company, True Fashionista, was nominated for the 2022 Small Business of the Year. She was also a 2022 Distinguished Entrepreneur finalist; and she was also part of the Bank of America Student Small Business Readiness Program.

Jennifer a contributing author to the bestselling *Slaying Southwest Florida: Stories of Powerful Women Leaving Their Mark.* She is also the host of *The Confident Entrepreneur* podcast and blog, and is a regular contributor to several local and national news outlets on business and her industry.

Fulfilling her love to give back to the community, Jennifer serves as the board president for Project Help in Naples. She also serves on the Greater Naples Chamber Board of Directors, on the Board of Trustees of The Village School of Naples, and on the Board of Directors of Sunrise Bay Toastmasters. She is also involved in the March of Dimes – having served as a chair for the March for Babies event – and in the Junior Women of Initiative program. Jennifer is a member of 100 Women Who Care in Southwest Florida.

She lives in Naples, Florida, with her husband and twins.

www.ingramcontent.com/pod-product-compliance
Lightning Source LLC
Chambersburg PA
CBHW061809070526
44586CB00024B/2778